First published 1982 by 'The Donkey Sanctuary'

© Elisabeth D. Svendsen. 1982

Photographs by: Nicholas Toyne
                  Ronald Busby
                  Roy Harrington

ISBN 1 85648 134 4

This edition published 1993 by The Promotional
Reprint Company Limited, Deacon House, 65 Old
Church Street, London SW3 5BS exclusively for
Bookmart Limited, Desford Road, Enderby, Leicester
LE9 5AD.

Printed in Spain.

AUTHOR'S NOTE

This book was written in 1982, when we had taken in 1400 donkeys into care. We have now taken in 5,690 donkeys and have nine farms. During this time many interesting cases have arrived, some humorous, some sad.

Our original intake sheets are still used, although more sophisticated and with a photograph of the donkey. Full medical records are transferred to our computer and the knowledge is stored and used in professional veterinary papers to further knowledge on this delightful animal; so necessary in the Third World where the donkey is so little cared for and so often abused.

I hope you enjoy the stories of twelve donkeys. Many of these donkeys can still be seen at the Donkey Sanctuary at Slade House Farm, Sidmouth, Devon.

Dr Elisabeth D. Svendsen, MBE, DVMS
Administrator
The Donkey Sanctuary,
Sidmouth, Devon EX10 0NU.

Tel.   (0395) 578222
Fax.   (0395) 759266

Also by Elisabeth D. Svendsen

Adult Books

Down Among the Donkeys
*Published in paperback in 1981 by Pan Book Ltd., Cavaye Place,
London SW10 9PG*
*Published in hardback by Robert Hale Ltd., Clerkenwell House,
Clerkenwell Green, London EC1R 0HT*

Childrens Books

The Story of Eeyore, the Naughtiest Donkey in the Sanctuary
The Donkeys Christmas Surprise
The Story of Suey, the Beach Donkey
More Adventures of Eeyore
Eeyore Helps the Children
Jacko, the Hurricane Donkey
All published by The Donkey Sanctuary

and

Eeyore and the Broken Collar
Tansy's Rescue
Eeyore Helps a Badger
The Great Escape
*Published by Piccolo Picture Books, Cavaye Place, London
SW10 9PG*

*All the above books are available from
The Donkey Sanctuary,
Sidmouth, Devon EX10 0NU*

Contents

Page

NAUGHTY FACE
THE DONKEY SANCTUARY, OTTERY ST. MARY, DEVON

SANCTUARY REF ....24........

THE DONKEY SANCTUARY
OTTERY ST. MARY, DEVON.

STALLION .... GELDING .... MARE ....Mare........

AGE ...4.+...................

NAME OF ANIMAL ...Naughty Face......

DATE OF ENTRY .....10.8.69.....................

SOURCE OF ENTRY ...Purchased from Mr Mogar...............................

....

GENERAL CONDITION ....Excellent.................................

....

....

VETERINARY REPORT .....Excellent..................................

....

....

FARRIERS REPORT .....Excellent..................................

....

WORMING RECORD DATES

14.8.69
14.10.69
For following dates see Veterinary Record

Naughty Face was previously owned by Mrs Svendsen but included in the
Sanctuary donkeys from 1974.

6

Naughty Face *"With the largest limpid brown eyes and softest black muzzle"*

NAUGHTY FACE

Naughty Face is not a Sanctuary donkey at all, but without her, none of the 1,300 donkeys who have found their way to safety in the Sanctuary could have arrived, so I feel she deserves the opening chapter!

I have always loved donkeys, ever since I was a child, and when we bought a hotel in Devon, I made sure the grounds were extensive enough for me to indulge in what I thought was going to be a part-time hobby.

Once we were settled, I was sitting glancing at the local newspaper when my eyes rested on one small advertisement: "Livestock for sale" was the heading, "Pedigree donkey mare for sale, Kennetbury Martha — apply Mr Mogar". The address was near, and the family piled into the car and went to see this 'pedigree donkey'! I had heard of thoroughbred everythings, but never donkeys, and wondered what she would look like. I can tell you she exceeded all my dreams. She was a proper grey donkey colour with the most beautiful clear cross marked on her back. Her bones were fine and she had legs almost like a racehorse. Her head was beautiful, with the largest limpid brown eyes and the softest black muzzle. We fell in love at once. She was superb and I could not wait to get her home. To add to my joy, it was explained that she was probably in foal to a stallion in the Donkey Breed Society stud book. I got the name and address of the Secretary of the D.B.S., determined to contact her on my return home.

I paid a cheque of £45.00 to Mr Mogar, who promised to deliver her when we had fenced off a paddock and built a stable.

I learnt a great deal from Susan Greenway, then Secretary of the D.B.S. — a society interested in all aspects of the donkey's life not **just** in breeding as the name suggests. Today it plays an important role in improving the image and condition of donkeys in this country, and I have the honour to be on its Council.

Back to Kennetbury Martha — her arrival was a much more significant event than I could possibly appreciate or foresee at the time. Down the ramp she trotted impertinently (did **she** know she was to be the first of over a thousand?) and into the paddock. I sat on the rails watching. Donkeys arriving in a new area are fairly predictable; they like to explore every corner and then return to indicate whether the new home is satisfactory or not! Kennetbury Martha returned and gave me such an enormous push with her head that I almost fell off the fence.

"Stop pushing me with that naughty face", I mumbled, restoring my dignity as best I could. I realised I had found a much better name for her than Kennetbury Martha, and Naughty Face she became.

Having approved her quarters, she examined her stable minutely, checked that her water, hay and straw were up to standard, had a long roll and decided she was home. We talked together for a long time and during my evening's work I kept making excuses to slip out and look at her!

Early morning is never the best time for hoteliers — we had not got to bed until 2 a.m. — but Naughty Face found the dawn lonely and her mournful brays brought less than appreciative comments from the rest of my family.

We soon bought her a companion, Angelina, and to my great joy Naughty Face produced a dear little foal I named 'Superdocious'.

I took Naughty Face to Devon County Show where she won the fifth prize. I could not have been more proud if I had won it myself, although I was not so sure I agreed with the judge that there could possibly be four donkeys better than she was!

As my love for donkeys grew, and turned from showing to helping those in distress, my love for Naughty Face never diminished, although it has had to be shared, and I was so proud of her on the many occasions when she called me out at the Sanctuary.

She always had a box in the yard near my window and when there was a donkey in trouble, it was always Naughty Face whose bray called me out. I am sure she knew my bedroom window, because as soon as the light went on, she stopped braying. She knew I was on my way. One particular summer night when all the donkeys, except the very sick, were out at grass, there was a tremendous thunderstorm. In the middle of the storm came the unmistakable braying. Someone must be in trouble. My husband and I dressed quickly. Naughty Face was calling from the valley that runs down to the sea, and we found her in the light of the big torch braying mournfully by Beth, a recent arrival, who, totally unexpectedly, had produced a foal!

Thanks to her help both were saved, and little 'Storm', as we named him, is fit and well today.

My donkey Naughty Face is still here at the farm. She is getting on in years now. I bought her in August 1969, but she is still as lovely as ever and never seems to get too jealous of my divided attention. After Superdocious, she had another foal called Delta, and they live happily together in their own donkey heaven.

HANSEL & GRETAL

THE DONKEY SANCTUARY, OTTERY ST. MARY, DEVON

SANCTUARY REF ...150.........

THE DONKEY SANCTUARY
OTTERY ST. MARY, DEVON.

STALLION .... GELDING .Gelding......... MARE ....

AGE ..4.......................

NAME OF ANIMAL ..Hansel..............

DATE OF ENTRY ...10.9.74........................

SOURCE OF ENTRY .Miss Philpin's donkey via Mr & Mrs Bloggs................

With 21 other donkeys. Companion of Gretal

GENERAL CONDITION ...This donkey is in extremis - showing severe distress

due to starvation.

VETERINARY REPORT ...His condition is appalling and he will be lucky to

live. No disease apparent.

FARRIERS REPORT ....Okay...............................

WORMING RECORD DATES

10.11.74
10. 1.75
For following dates see Veterinary Record

SANCTUARY REF ..151...........

THE DONKEY SANCTUARY
OTTERY ST. MARY, DEVON.

STALLION .... GELDING .... MARE ..Mare..........

AGE ....4.....................

NAME OF ANIMAL ..Gretal...............

DATE OF ENTRY ...10.9.74........................

SOURCE OF ENTRY .....Miss Philpin's donkey via Mr & Mrs Bloggs............

With 21 other donkeys. Companion of Hansel

GENERAL CONDITION ...Very, very poor - breathing laboured and heavy........

VETERINARY REPORT ...A walking skelton, full of lice, starved almost to....

death.

FARRIERS REPORT ....Slightly overgrown..........................

WORMING RECORD DATES

10.11.74
10.1.75
For following dates see Veterinary Record

10

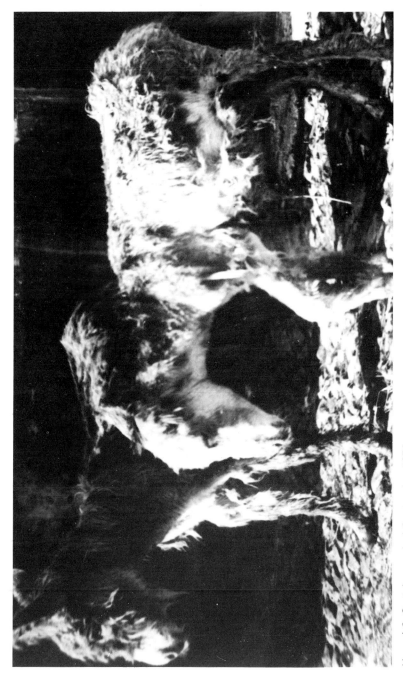

Hansel & Gretal on arrival September 1974

HANSEL & GRETAL

After the death of Miss Philpin and my surprise legacy of 204 donkeys, one of the worst jobs was tracing the animals that were not at the Sanctuary in Reading. I was very soon informed of the whereabouts of one group of twenty-two who had apparently been cared for by a couple to whom I shall, for obvious reasons, refer as Mr and Mrs Bloggs. They were boarding them out for Miss Philpin at a cost of £2.00 per animal per week and they wanted the large sum of money they said Miss Philpin owed them.

I called round to see them and they agreed that I could send a lorry round to collect the donkeys. I called at a difficult time, as they were just putting Sunday lunch on the table, so I did not see the donkeys which were in a field some distance away. I knew I would see them on their arrival the next day.

At the time, Judith Forbes, who was running the Countryside Park three miles from my home, was renting me a large modern barn for the larger loads of arrivals, and it was she who phoned me from there; normally a very calm person, she sounded desperate on the telephone.

"Betty, the wagon's arrived; please come at once. It's absolutely terrible; I just can't believe my eyes. The donkeys are in the most appalling condition."

I jumped into my car with Rosalind de Wesselow, who was one of the five Trustees of the Donkey Sanctuary and we drove to Farway. The whole group were in the most appalling condition, but two tiny ones were huddled together, barely able to stand, heads down, eyes dull with starvation, walking skeletons covered in matted hair, full of lice and sores.

We had to carry them into a little stable that Mrs Forbes immediately offered us. We gently laid them down on the deep straw. I just could not believe people could allow any animal to get into such a state. I was so angry I rang the R.S.P.C.A. and asked them to come out at once, as I was determined to bring a prosecution against the Bloggs.

I named the two little donkeys Hansel and Gretal, as for them it must have been an indescribable time, like the situation in the fairy tale. The vet's report on Hansel was: "This donkey is in extremis — showing severe distress due to starvation. His condition is appalling and he will be lucky to live. No disease apparent." On Gretal the comments were: "Very, very poor — breathing laboured and heavy, a walking skeleton, full of lice, starved almost to death."

Their first good moment must have been when they felt a gentle hand by their mouths offering a warm, nourishing mash. This must have been the first proper food they had had for very many months. The answer to treating such starvation is "little and often", and for many days and nights they and three others from the group had to be hand fed. Gradually their strength began to return, and after nine days they could stand unaided. Only then were they fit to be gently brought back to my

12

house where it was so much easier to do the night feeds that were still so essential. They were still terrified of being handled, but they were beginning to know us. As they improved, I was able to start the long job of gently clipping away the matted hair and getting rid of the deeply embedded lice. Even though I wore a headsquare and tightly fitting clothes, there was still a ring of lice around the bath when I got out. Ugh!

It was while I was busily employed clipping that Julie Courtney turned up for an interview as Secretary. Now many years later she is the Assistant Administrator, still helping to do the donkey work!

With the vet's help the sores were treated and began to heal and Hansel and Gretal began to enjoy life. They had to be rugged up every night as the evenings got colder, and we fitted an infra red light over them to keep them warm. It was such a joy to see them begin to enjoy life, and the first time they were able to go out in the paddock for a little exercise, I nearly cried. We always have a sanded area, as donkeys love to roll, and I always sprinkle louse powder in it, so every donkey wriggle helps with the constant enemy. Hansel and Gretal spent the first few minutes rolling over and over in the sand, so obviously appreciating the back scratching sensation and rolling into each other regularly. Then up they got and, to my joy, broke into a trot round the paddock.

After putting Hansel and Gretal in their stable on that terrible day of arrival, I had written to Mr Bloggs telling him what I thought of his care of the donkeys and adding that, through the R.S.P.C.A., we intended to bring a prosecution.

To my horror on receipt of the letter, he phoned me and said he was going to take the donkeys back again and wanted their address. He was sure we wouldn't pay the money Miss Philpin had owed and was most unpleasant. I told him the donkeys were not at my address, but were elsewhere, but he said he was coming anyway and would find them.

I was terrified that he would try to take them away again and rang the police who were wonderful, particularly when I showed them Hansel and Gretal! For two days the police were always near, until I realised that the man would not carry out his threat.

The law took its course, and in December the case came up. With the photographs we had taken, our Veterinary Surgeon and the R.S.P.C.A. officer, we arrived at the Court. When I heard Mr & Mrs Bloggs' evidence I just couldn't believe it! The donkeys, according to them, had been groomed, fed and cared for daily. Fortunately, the photographs showed the truth, and the couple were found guilty under the Protection of Animals Act 1911 and fined the maximum penalty of £50. Considering that four of the group of 22 died within two years as a direct result of the starvation they had been subjected to, it did not seem a very heavy fine.

Gretal progressed steadily, but Hansel took much, much longer. After two years with us, he seemed set to develop fully, but then we nearly had a disaster. Although a gelding, he still had male instincts and one day tried to ride Gretal. To our horror, he dislocated his hip and the vet had quite a job to help him. Since that date, he has been a little more cautious, and they both live in the special care unit at Slade House Farm. They have their own beautiful stable, the cost of which is borne by a subscriber in memory of his sister who was killed in a car crash. They are not as soft and gentle as some of the donkeys — those four early years have left their mark — but they are certainly enjoying life and deserve every moment of happiness they can get.

Hansel & Gretal 8 years later

ALFRED

DONKEY ADMISSION SHEET FOR THE DONKEY SANCTUARY, SIDMOUTH, DEVON

Computer Entry Date ....

DONKEY ADMISSION SHEET FOR THE DONKEY SANCTUARY, SIDMOUTH, DEVON

NAME: ....Alfred........................ REF NO: .....117.....................

D.O.E. ....24.7.74....................... AGE: ....6...................

SEX: ......Gelding................. IF STALLION, GELDING DATE: ....

COLOUR AND DESCRIPTION: .....Very large, brown..................................

....

....

....

SINGLE/COMPANIONS: ....With Miss V. Philpin's donkeys.......................

....

....

....

SOURCE OF ENTRY: ......Miss Philpin's Sanctuary...............................

....

....

....

IF VIA D.S.I. INSPECTOR: ....

GENERAL CONDITION ON ARRIVAL: Good

MEDICAL HISTORY/BACKGROUND, ETC:

FIRST VET REPORT: Reasonable but lungworm on test

FARRIER REPORT: Feet in need of attention

WEIGHT ON ARRIVAL: ...260 kilos.....

FIRST WORMED: ......28.7.74........

SECOND WORMED: .....28.9.74........

FIRST VACCINATION: ...28.7.74......

SECOND VACCINATION: ...29.8.74......

For following dates see Veterinary Record

15

Alfred on arrival July 1974

ALFRED

One of the donkeys picked up from the Reading Sanctuary after the death of Miss Philpin was one I named 'Alfred' after Alfred the Great. At that time he was the biggest donkey we had taken into the Sanctuary and apart from his hooves, which were badly in need of a trim, he was in fairly good condition.

Although large, he could be described as almost elegant. He had excellent manners, always carried himself well and was a perfect gentleman with the farrier.

Shortly after his arrival my ideas for putting handicapped children and donkeys together for their mutual benefit got under way and Alfred, partly because of his size and partly because of his good manners, was chosen for the trial. He proved absolutely wonderful. The children adored Alfred and Alfred adored the children.

In those days, before we built our centre, we would take the donkeys out to the children at their schools. We had a wonderful team including Alfred, Violetta, Solo and Pedro. An excellent horsewoman called Vanadia Sandon-Humphries had joined me and she agreed to take charge of the riding on the visits. Volunteers from the village of Salcombe Regis and Sidmouth joined us to make a team, and because our farm was Slade House we decided to name the new charity The Slade Centre. We visited five schools in the Exeter, Exmouth, Honiton districts and each visit was quite a day for us all!

The children shrieked with joy when the wagon ramp came down and the donkeys came out. To many it was the event of the week. Noddy (as we all affectionately called Vanadia) was patience itself, tacking up the donkeys and organising the rides. We were very careful to give the donkeys plenty of rest and Alfred found one way to get his reward.

We had not realised that Violetta was in season and were happily relaxing having a cup of coffee with the staff at Withycombe House, Exmouth, when one of the children said, "Look, Miss. Alfred's having a ride."

We all looked at the donkeys, loosely tied and grazing, still tacked up under the shade of the hedge, and there was Alfred, front hooves neatly tucked into Violetta's stirrup, attending to his male instincts! Although a gelding, no one seemed to have told Alfred, but he was most dignified in his retreat!

The children's joy turned to sadness in the winter when the rides had to stop, but in December 1978, the Slade Centre opened, with its super play area and riding arena designed for the comfort of donkeys and children alike. Now the rides can take place 6 days a week, 52 weeks a year.

There is a team of fifteen donkeys, who are all specially trained and who really enjoy giving rides, but Alfred is **still** the favourite.

Only last month, the Principal, Mrs Pat Feather, called me over and told me a fantastic story authenticated by staff of the visiting special school and our own senior staff. Alfred was the second in line of five donkeys giving rides to children from Ellen Tinkham School. The children were severely disabled, and to encourage them to bend and to co-ordinate arm and eye, one of the many games we use had been set up.

Propped against the rail on the left hand side of the arena were a number of addressed envelopes and on the other side was a letter box. The child, on donkey back, had to stop the donkey, pick up the letter, ride around the arena, and post it at the other side.

Alfred's rider was severely crippled, and despite very real attempts the child could not pick up the envelope. After the child had failed at the third attempt, Alfred turned his head round and grasped the envelope firmly in his teeth then, to everyone's amazement, he carried his rider to the letter box and stopped with the envelope only inches from the hole! Who says donkeys are not intelligent? After a ride, each child is encouraged to love their donkey, and Alfred had a very special 'love' that day.

I always feel that the handicapped child looks on the donkeys as handicapped horses and they can form very real associations with them. I think it wonderful that the donkeys, having been rescued themselves, can in turn give help to handicapped children and I know they enjoy it. No donkey is ever forced to work. If they appear at all unwilling, they are immediately changed, but this rarely happens. The affection really is mutual, and in all the years of work and thousands of rides, only one child has ever been injured and that through no fault of the donkey.

Alfred the Great is truly named.

Alfred outside the Slade Centre 1982

SMARTIE
THE DONKEY SANCTUARY, OTTERY ST. MARY, DEVON

SANCTUARY REF .....240........

THE DONKEY SANCTUARY
OTTERY ST. MARY, DEVON.

STALLION .... GELDING .... MARE .....Mare.........

AGE .....2...................

NAME OF ANIMAL .....Smartie...............

DATE OF ENTRY .....9.4.73....................

SOURCE OF ENTRY .....Dealer...

....

GENERAL CONDITION .....Very poor. Emaciated. Collapsed within 12 hours.....
of arrival.

VETERINARY REPORT .....Malnutrition. Suggest glucose feed hourly..........
Donkey not likely to survive.

FARRIERS REPORT .....Feet reasonable..................................

WORMING RECORD DATES

9.6.73
9.8.73
For following dates see Veterinary Record

20

Smartie after the farrier's first visit

SMARTIE

No book of my favourite donkeys would be complete without devoting at least one chapter to Smartie.

Her arrival had been a dreadful shock. She had been delivered as an apparently normal donkey in perfect health. At the time of her arrival I was the South West Area Representative for the Donkey Breed Society and a member had asked if I would help to get a family donkey. As no members had a suitable animal, I saw one advertised in the local paper and arranged for her to be delivered to me so that I could make sure she would be a sound purchase for the member. I was not there when she was delivered but when I arrived, I was disturbed to find I could not get near her; she was obviously terrified and looked thin and scruffy. I decided to leave her until she had settled after the journey, and left her feed, water and hay in the paddock. My husband and I were wakened at dawn by the braying of the other donkeys in the field, however, and, to our horror, we could see her lying motionless in the field, the other donkeys gathered round her. Quickly we dressed and stood by her side — she was barely breathing. To our surprise and horror, the two of us were able to lift her and we gently carried her to a small shed by the back door. Poor Smartie was too ill to be frightened now and lay, eyes shut, while we rugged her up and fixed up an infra red lamp for warmth. While my husband rang for the vet, I spooned glucose and water down her throat. All that long day we continued the treatment. The injections given by the vet, the warmth and nourishment very slowly took effect. She began to take a little more interest in life. I knelt by her and moving the blanket began to brush her gently. Great handfuls of lice infected hair came away and sore after sore was revealed.

By evening, after managing a little bran mash, she stood up, and it was a unique moment for both of us. My son Clive came in and said, "She looks quite different now she's brushed out — a real smartie," and that's how 'Smartie' got her name.

I never paid a penny for her. I had a most traumatic meeting with the dealer who had advertised her. I got him to the house and showed her to him. He was a great actor and seemed genuinely surprised.

"I just can't understand it," he said, scratching his head. "I got her in the market and she seemed the best of the bunch."

I shuddered to think what the rest had looked like.

I told him I was going to bring a prosecution, but realised I was on shaky ground, as he had apparently bought her only a few days before he had delivered her, but the threat was enough.

"That's not the donkey I delivered here," he said firmly. "I don't want any money for her — you can keep her — never seen her before!"

And he slammed out of the stable and drove away at full speed.

She had arrived in April 1973, before the Sanctuary had got under way, and I was appalled at her general condition and that of her feet! Obviously she had not had the farrier for some time, and her feet had grown longer and longer until they had begun to turn up at the front, making it very painful for her to walk. It took the farrier almost a year to get them right. It is impossible to correct such severe deformities straight away, as the tendons have stretched at the back of the donkey's leg and much pain and damage can be caused by trying to attain the correct shape too soon. In view of her terrible condition, Smartie moved very little during her first months with me; in a way this gave her feet time to recover.

I was delighted by the way her character changed. She soon welcomed me with a bray every time I came into her stable and she became very gentle. We knew each other so well, that I could visit her when she was lying down and she never got up! A great honour!

She amazed the vet by her recovery. Soon she began to put on weight and began to lose her skeleton-like appearance. In fact, she began to put on rather too much weight and I began to feel a little suspicious.

One night, as we gently talked and touched each other in our nightly ritual that all the donkeys love, I noticed a definite movement in the now bulging stomach! I laid my hand on her side and nearly had it pushed off by a hard kicking little hoof somewhere in there.

"Oh, Smartie," I said, holding her head in my hands and looking into her beautiful limpid eyes. "Smartie, you're going to have a baby. Thank God you got here in time."

I can swear a tear spilled out of those lovely eyes to mingle with mine dropping on that dear soft muzzle.

I couldn't leave her stable as her time drew near. She had been with me almost a year. Gestation for a donkey is between 12 and 15 months, so I knew she must be nearly due. Most donkeys prefer to have their foals alone and can in fact stop the first stages of labour for quite a long period of time if they are disturbed. However, it is only too easy to lose the foal if the mare is weak, as the membrane bag in which it is born can be very tough, and the foal can suffocate if the bag does not break naturally, or if the mother does not bite it open. For this reason, obviously, I kept a very close eye on Smartie. I need not have bothered to set the alarm and visit her hourly. An enormous braying jerked me into consciousness at 2.30 a.m. on June 20th, 1974; rushing to Smartie's stable, I found her in the last stages of labour, panting desperately.

"It's all right, Smartie," I said, and she immediately calmed. Seconds later out slithered the foal.

He didn't need any help. With a few hefty movements, the baby emerged from the bag, shook his head and reached out towards Smartie, who had turned to look in proud amazement.

"You've done it Smartie," I cried in joy. "It's a super little colt. What shall we call him?"

And to my surprise, Smartie named him. Throwing up her head she gave a triumphant bray, "Eeyore, Eeyore," and so we named the little foal who was to become the naughtiest donkey in the Sanctuary.

The story has a very sad ending; on the 20th March 1981 Smartie was found dead in her stable. She had had almost eight years of happiness in her life and the post mortem was inconclusive. One can only assume that eventually her near death due to starvation had shortened her expected life span.

Fortunately for Eeyore, he had already made firm friends with Frosty, Pancho and Ruff and he was old enough and strong enough not to be too much affected.

I still miss Smartie. I wish I could tell you that she is still alive, and show you an up-to-date photograph of her. She is no longer with us, but happily many of the other donkeys pictured here are alive and enjoying their safe refuge at the Sanctuary.

Smartie and Eeyore August 1974

EEYORE

THE DONKEY SANCTUARY, OTTERY ST. MARY, DEVON

SANCTUARY REF ...241...........

THE DONKEY SANCTUARY
OTTERY ST. MARY, DEVON.

STALLION .... GELDING ...3.7.75 (10 months) MARE ....

AGE ..Born 20.8.74...............

NAME OF ANIMAL ..Eeyore..............

DATE OF ENTRY ..20.6.74........................

SOURCE OF ENTRY ..Born to Smartie...

....

GENERAL CONDITION ....

....

....

VETERINARY REPORT ....

....

....

FARRIERS REPORT ....

....

WORMING RECORD DATES

20.10.74
20.12.74
For following dates see Veterinary Record

"Is anybody looking?"

"Now I'm in the garden I'll try a rose"

EEYORE

Of all the foals that have been born in the Sanctuary, I think Eeyore gave me most joy. It was such a joint effort, and Smartie was so generous in her sharing of him and together we watched him grow. He soon found the milk bar, and was greedily suckling almost before Smartie had finished her congratulatory bucket of hot bran mash! He was very sturdy and the most beautiful shade of grey. Even at birth, the cross on his back was clearly marked. This cross is said to have been given to all donkeys by Jesus who rode into Jerusalem on an ass, the name given many years ago to the donkey.

Eeyore was a little mischief! Poor Smartie, she only had to lie down in the field to rest and he would nudge her, push her and try, frequently and noisily, to jump right over her! It was a good job she was fully recovered, as he was into everything. I was frequently called by a desperate Smartie as Eeyore had got under the fence and was happily exploring pastures new, with Smartie helpless on the other side. When I tried to guide him back, he would playfully kick his heels up and I really had to watch him after a while — he could give you quite a hard, well directed thump!

Fortunately, he could only have been conceived just before Smartie had arrived with us and had been able to take advantage of the special care and treatment his mother had had. He was a perfect example of a donkey, and, in the early days, I never realised what mischief he would get up to.

The farrier, John Craddock, was the first to appreciate what we were rearing. To do Smartie's hooves, he would bend down with his back to her head and, grasping her hoof between his knees, just clip away the excess horn and then file the hoof to the correct shape. It took quite a deal of concentration and he tended to ignore the dear little foal nuzzling round him until — "Ouch!," the hoof was dropped and John's hands shot to his posterior! Eeyore had found a new game which was much more fun than teasing Smartie.

From that day our trouble started. The Sanctuary was now formed and growing fast, and Eeyore had a large number of new friends to play with. I think he enjoyed the move to Slade House Farm more than anyone. Being led on to a lorry brings back real memories of terror to many donkeys, and Smartie certainly felt fear and stopped, trembling, her feet on the ramp.

"It's all right, Smartie," I said. "Only a few miles to a lovely new home," but still she hesitated. Then 'clatter, clatter, clatter' and past trotted Eeyore — up the ramp to gaze down at his mother as if to say, "What on earth's the matter?" Smartie hesitated no longer and went up into the box; at this, just as the doors were closing, Eeyore shot past us all, down the ramp and into the yard!

Laughing, we went down and herded him up. It seemed so easy — half way! Then with no effort at all he hunched himself up with all four little legs together, leapt over the side of the ramp and off up the drive!

"Oh, Eeyore," we all shouted, but he was off.

Smartie's anxious face was peering out as we shut up the box and went after him.

He had stopped, just out of sight, and was pretending to eat some roses from the neighbour's garden. As soon as we got near — off he moved again; it was like playing the childhood game 'black puddings' or 'grandmother's footsteps'!

Using our 'superior' intelligence we eventually caught him and this time carried him right on to the lorry, to be greeted by a very tight-lipped Smartie!

The new farm was heaven for Eeyore. Compared with Salston Close, where he had been born and where the Sanctuary originated, it was a donkeys' delight. We fenced the fields carefully so that each area had a patch of woodland — donkeys love the trace elements they get from bark — and there was even wild garlic which reputedly helps with the parasite problem.

Eeyore, Smartie and the rest of the group went into a large airy barn at night and on the first night I sank gratefully into bed knowing that all were safely shut up for the night. I was, however, to be further educated! Eeyore found a way to open the door! I had latched it firmly, but from little teeth marks round the latch the next morning, I learnt what had happened. Sometime during that night, Eeyore had let himself out, and Maud, a very elderly donkey who had assumed a type of 'Grandma' role, managed to follow him before the door swung shut again. Off trotted Eeyore determined to explore his new surroundings!

I was awakened by Smartie's desperate braying, and gradually I realised who was missing. I had to shut the top of the stable door as well when I went to look for Eeyore and Maud, or a desperate Smartie would have launched herself over the top! I stood quietly by the track and listened. Yes — there in the woodland area was the mournful sepulchral bray of Maud. Armed with a torch and accompanied by my son Clive, I followed the sounds. I soon found a, by now, very grateful Eeyore and Maud lost in the woods, and led them home!

By the next morning Eeyore was apparently quite happy to graze peacefully, but I got a little angry that the donkeys' water butt was empty.

Herb had been with me for years and assured me he had filled it that morning and that the bung at the bottom must have come out. He refilled it carefully, and all was well until tea time when, once again, the butt was empty. This time we put the donkeys away for the night after refilling the butt and it was still full of cool clear water in the morning. Next day I idly leant on the fence watching the donkeys enjoy their early morning roll; and then Eeyore left the others and sidled up to the trough. He didn't want a drink, oh no — his little teeth closed around the plug — he braced his little hooves and pulled — and stood in delight watching the water run between his legs and down the field!

Water had a fatal fascination for him. Later, the nursery group used to go out with the geriatrics in the paddock by the intensive care unit where there was a lovely shallow duck pond with gently sloping edges. One day there was a shout from the yard staff, and we all had to rush out and rescue Nellie, an elderly donkey, who had somehow got herself into the middle of the pond and couldn't get out. She seemed fine after her ordeal, and not a bit concerned, and we thought little more of the incident until one afternoon a little later. I was in the office, and through my window, I could see the geriatrics. This time Gertrude was by the side of the pond dozing quietly, with her ears twitching. Up came Eeyore. He was standing very close to Gertrude and seemed to be leaning on her. I sprang from my seat and flung the window open shouting "EEYORE!" but it was too late. As though in slow motion, Gertrude tottered on the edge and then 'SPLASH'! It took three of us to get her out. Eeyore was confined to stables for the rest of the day!

Eeyore's antics always appealed to the children. A school near Bristol, Compton Dando, had taken a great interest in him and their joy when they visited him was evident — particularly when he galloped off with one of their bobble caps.

I decided his stories would make good children's books with a little education squeezed in, and this has turned out to be the most marvellous fund-raiser for the Sanctuary. By publishing myself and cutting the costs, I made nearly £40,000 for the Sanctuary in just three years of writing, and that amount has more than doubled by now. All the stories are completely true with just a little artist's licence in places and perhaps a little guesswork, particularly where the badger Eeyore brought in was concerned. He was certainly always at the gate until the badger had recovered enough to leave us, and I'm pretty sure he had plenty to do with it! His only failure was when we tried to train him for the Slade Centre to help the handicapped children: His sense of humour proved too great, and he couldn't resist pinching the children's toys and galloping off with them.

Today, with his friends, he is here at Slade House. He has developed a growth on his shoulder which will have to be removed if it gets any bigger but otherwise he is well, so watch out for him! His latest hobby is handbag collecting from adoring, unsuspecting visitors!

TIMOTHY

DONKEY ADMISSION SHEET FOR THE DONKEY SANCTUARY, SIDMOUTH, DEVON

Computer Entry Date ....

DONKEY ADMISSION SHEET FOR THE DONKEY SANCTUARY, SIDMOUTH, DEVON

NAME: ...Timothy............... REF NO: ...365...............

D.O.E. ...5.7.76............... AGE: ...25...............

SEX: ...Gelding........... IF STALLION, GELDING DATE: ....

COLOUR AND DESCRIPTION: .....Small, grey, small muzzle, mutilated ears......

....

....

....

SINGLE/COMPANIONS: ....Single................................

....

....

....

SOURCE OF ENTRY: ....Horse & Pony Protection Trust Society...............

....

....

....

IF VIA D.S.I. INSPECTOR: ....

GENERAL CONDITION ON ARRIVAL: Extremely nervous and very difficult to handle

MEDICAL HISTORY/BACKGROUND, ETC: Ears severed - Major temperament problem

FIRST VET REPORT: Heart and lungs ok.
Main muscle in both ears severed by carving knife -
improvement impossible.

FARRIER REPORT: Reasonable

WEIGHT ON ARRIVAL: ..Not weighed....

FIRST WORMED: .....8.7.76...........

SECOND WORMED: ....9.9.76...........

FIRST VACCINATION: ..19.7.76........

SECOND VACCINATION: 23.8.76
.... For following dates see Veterinary Record

Weight at 14.3.77   384 lbs

31

Timothy on arrival July 1976

Timothy shaking hands with Herb!

TIMOTHY

If you are at all squeamish, don't read the first part of this story, because I still can't recount it without shuddering.

Some six years ago, Timothy was a happy normal gelding in his mid-twenties. A reasonable age for a donkey — we have them in the Sanctuary up to the age of fifty. We are told that he was given as a present to a young village boy when he gained his eleven plus exam. The boy had always wanted a donkey and his father already had a small well-fenced paddock near the main road.

When Timothy arrived there was great delight amongst the family and the boy visited Timothy every possible moment and they both got on really well. Then one evening the indescribable happened. A small group of boys from the village school, who had failed their exam, had become very jealous. As the boy was so attached to Timothy, they decided to attack him and five of the boys, one armed with a carving knife, crept up to his field one evening. Timothy had no reason to be afraid of the boys and had no sense of danger, but his terror at what happened next can still be seen in his eyes. With four holding him down, one of the boys sliced savagely through one ear and then the other. In agonised terror Timothy flung them off and was still blundering desperately around the field, blood flowing down his eyes, when the unsuspecting owner arrived with his evening carrot. You can imagine the scene. First a vet came and managed to deaden the pain and then came the police, but because the boys were so young a prosecution was not possible. The boy was heartbroken — Timothy would not let him anywhere near — rearing and kicking at the approach of anyone. His father was desperate and rang The Horse and Pony Protection Trust Society who collected Timothy and took him away from his scene of terror. They tended his wounds and, after a very difficult period of time, got a local farmer to put him in his field with some horses. Timothy, however, was no longer capable of being sociable with either people or animals, and after a while the farmer had to advise the Horse and Pony Protection Trust Society that it was impossible for anyone to keep him. They realised they had a major temperament problem on their hands and rang us to see if we would take him as we had so much experience with donkeys.

When we unloaded him from the box my heart sank. We saw with horror his poor damaged ears; his lips were drawn back, his eyes red and angry and he was obviously emotionally disturbed. Gently we put him in a loosebox, took off his halter and left him in peace with hay and a bran mash. When I went in to collect the bucket half an hour later, I thought my end had come. Timothy attacked me, not with his hindlegs (which one gets used to) but with his front hooves, rearing up and trying to hoof me under, eyes blazing, teeth bared. It's hard to appear calm on these occasions, but I knew I must not let him sense any fear from me and I managed to slip out minus the bucket!

After that it was always what we call a 'two man box' — one to put in the feed and the other to ward Timothy off!

My heart bled for him. I was sure I would have lost trust in people too and we tried every trick we knew to gain his confidence. Herb, who had been with me since the Sanctuary opened, coped with him best but even he made little progress.

Knowing how all donkeys are better in company, we tried introducing him to other geldings, but he cared for them no more than for people and we frequently ended up rescuing the other gelding from the 'pairing box'. I was in despair. Suddenly it seemed the only answer was to be the ultimate one — to put him to sleep; to erase forever the terrible memories.

Then the miracle happened. Two very fat chocolate donkeys called Henry and Henrietta had come in. As Henry had been showing signs of extreme fatigue they were in the next stable to Timothy. One night on my evening rounds, I found Henry lying down, barely breathing, having suffered a massive heart attack. I ran in and phoned for our vet, whose practice was in Exeter, and then back to the stable armed with rugs to try to keep him warm till help arrived. As I knelt beside him, massaging his heart to try to encourage the very weak beat, Henrietta became a real nuisance, even standing on Henry's inert form in an endeavour to share what she thought was a pleasant stroking. I had no choice but to push her, protesting, into the long corridor, and she promptly vanished from view. By the time the vet arrived, Henry was unconscious and, despite injections and all the vets could do, we lost him. It always upsets me to lose a donkey, particularly when I don't feel they have had long enough to enjoy a well-earned rest or retirement. As I stumbled into the corridor half blinded with tears, I stopped in amazement. Timothy's head was extended over the door and gently nuzzling him was Henrietta! I just couldn't believe it! They both ignored me as I gently opened Timothy's door, and Henrietta walked into his stable calmly and continued the nuzzling.

The next morning Herb appeared with the most enormous grin on his face. In his soft Devonshire accent he said, "He'm got him a little maid and tiz a changed dunkey."

So it was. From that moment Timothy changed. Anyone could walk in his box. Helped by Henrietta, he began to accept tit-bits, and his attack with the front hooves was turned into a morning hoof shake with Herb.

After Timothy and Henrietta had spent a few days together, we decided to let them out in the yard and with some trepidation, I opened the door. Henrietta led the way, followed by a quiet Timothy, and together they explored every corner of the big yard. Having enjoyed an hour's excercise, they returned to their isolation stable, and from that day they were allowed a regular period of time outside. As soon as Henrietta's isolation period was over, we took them up to one of the fields, and for two days they had the private use of it, but they were able to talk to the donkeys in the next field over the fence. Henrietta was very firm with Timothy, and at the first sign of bared teeth she would push him away from the donkey he was talking to! On the third day together, we allowed them into a group of donkeys, and now, with Henrietta always near him, he is living a happy, peaceful life again. He seems to have forgiven man for his inhumanity and would we, or could we, all do the same?

Timothy July 1982

BUFFALO

DONKEY ADMISSION SHEET FOR THE DONKEY SANCTUARY, SIDMOUTH, DEVON

Computer Entry Date ....

DONKEY ADMISSION SHEET FOR THE DONKEY SANCTUARY, SIDMOUTH, DEVON

NAME: ...Buffalo...................... REF NO: ...457..................

D.O.E. ...2.2.77.................. AGE: ...30....................

SEX: ...Gelding............ IF STALLION, GELDING DATE: ....

COLOUR AND DESCRIPTION: ...Brown; very large; long hair; long ears...............

....

....

....

SINGLE/COMPANIONS: ...Blupy 456, Bonanza 458, Bobby B. 459..............

....

....

....

SOURCE OF ENTRY: ...R.S.P.C.A. Blackpool...............................

....

....

....

IF VIA D.S.I. INSPECTOR: ....

GENERAL CONDITION ON ARRIVAL: Fair

MEDICAL HISTORY/BACKGROUND, ETC: Beach donkey

FIRST VET REPORT: Fair

FARRIER REPORT: Good

WEIGHT ON ARRIVAL: ...295 kilos.....

FIRST WORMED: ......5.9.77............

SECOND WORMED: ......5.11.77..........

FIRST VACCINATION: ....4.9.77.........

SECOND VACCINATION: ...4.10.77........

For following dates See Veterinary Record

36

BUFFALO

Buffalo **must** be one of the biggest donkeys around, and he certainly must have the biggest ears in the business!

Thousands of years ago, when donkeys and horses lived wild in Africa and Asia, the stronger horses tended to push the donkeys off the lusher pastures, so the donkeys took to the hills and mountains where, although the grazing was much poorer, they could at least graze peacefully. This made communication difficult, and this appears to be the reason for the donkey's penetrating voice to call with and large ears to hear with. If this is so, then Buffalo could go up the highest mountain and still hear his friends!

He came to us in September 1977 and was the four hundred and fifty-seventh entry to the Sanctuary. He arrived with three friends Blupy, Bonanza and Bobby: all had been working on Blackpool beach for (excuse the expression) donkey's years!

Blackpool is a unique area for donkeys. It has its own charter that goes back over 100 years and is the only town that is not obliged to abide by the special laws relating to the working of equines. This is because it has cared for donkeys for so many years and the facilities there are so good.

I have seen over 100 donkeys working on the beach at one time. Each operator has his own stand, and during the season these are moved in rotation, so a fair deal for both donkey and operators is achieved.

Provided beach donkeys are properly looked after, in summer and winter, and their owners licensed and inspected, I do not oppose donkeys giving rides. So many people remember the very special times in their childhood when on holiday they had a donkey ride; a memorable event. Given proper conditions and no loads over 8 stone, the donkeys do not seem to suffer — indeed many enjoy it!

All beach donkeys are regularly inspected by the Riding Establishment Acts Committee, the R.S.P.C.A. and ourselves. We now have 56 inspectors watching markets, beaches and following up cases of cruelty to donkeys.

It was through the R.S.P.C.A. that Buffalo and his friends joined us. They were all in their thirties and the beach operator decided they deserved a good retirement! He contacted Inspector Matthews of the R.S.P.C.A. who rang us and of course we agreed they deserved a happy home with us.

When the lorry doors opened I couldn't believe the size of Buffalo! His feet were over twice the size of the average donkey's and as my eyes went upwards, there was the most enormous shaggy body, crowned with a superb head and the most enormous ears.

"Both ears up"

"First one collapses"

"They lie at right angles to his head"

Every new arrival at the Sanctuary is given a name and a number and, at the time of Buffalo's arrival, we were buying made up 'cow collars'. These were yellow and were designed to fit a cow's neck.

"Goodness," I muttered as I tried in vain to get the collar around his neck. "We need one big enough for a buffalo," and so he got his name. Actually he did us a great favour as we rang the factory, Daltons. In future they sent the collar material in rolls; this was much cheaper, and we make them up ourselves to neck size. We can then fit on the buckles and with a small soldering iron, burn in the donkey's name and number. Collars are vitally important, as we have so many animals. First there is the colour code — white for stallions, yellow for mares and red for geldings. Secondly, it is easy to see the donkey's name and number; every new arrival also has a blue collar to show that he/she is in isolation; this is removed after the six week period. We always have to be careful that stallions are never accidentally mixed with mares before they are castrated. We have enough problems without further little ones!

Back to Buffalo — he is such a softy — it's almost impossible to describe him. When he is being groomed and you bend down to brush his legs, slowly he begins to lean on you — a beatific expression on his face! Only the strongest can take his weight, and I certainly don't qualify for that, usually collapsing in an undignified heap to be nudged up by Buffalo — an enquiring expression on his face.

The first time John Craddock, our farrier, saw him he put down his file and slowly walked around him with a delighted grin on his face.

"Now that's what I call a donkey," he said. "Not half so far to bend as usual, but is he good?"

He soon found out. Buffalo enjoyed his pedicure thoroughly and stood patiently, even lifting his enormous feet towards John as he bent to his task.

His only problem seems to be the enormous size of his ears. When he gets tired, the muscle needed to hold them up seems to sag, and slowly, like great handlebars, first one collapses, then the other, until finally they lie at right angles to his head!

In the winter, when all the donkeys are stabled, he has an enormous advantage — standing in the second row behind one of the smaller donkeys in the group, he casually leans over and helps himself to nuts and hay.

He has earned and deserved the name 'Gentle Giant' here, and is dearly loved and petted by all the children who visit. He still bears the white hairs on his flanks, caused by the saddle rubbing, but with Buffalo I look on this as a mark of honour — the donkey's highest award for his years of happily carrying and giving delight to thousands of children.

SUEY

DONKEY ADMISSION SHEET FOR THE DONKEY SANCTUARY, SIDMOUTH, DEVON

Computer Entry Date ....

DONKEY ADMISSION SHEET FOR THE DONKEY SANCTUARY, SIDMOUTH, DEVON

NAME: ...Suey........................... REF NO: ...281.....................

D.O.E. ...29.6.75................... AGE: ...25+......................

SEX: ...Mare................. IF STALLION, GELDING DATE: ....

COLOUR AND DESCRIPTION: ...Dark brown/black..

....

....

....

SINGLE/COMPANIONS: ....Single.................................

....

....

....

SOURCE OF ENTRY: ....From beach operator.......................

....

....

....

IF VIA D.S.I. INSPECTOR: ....

GENERAL CONDITION ON ARRIVAL: Thin and very little strength

MEDICAL HISTORY/BACKGROUND, ETC: Beach donkey - collapsed on beach

FIRST VET REPORT: Fair

FARRIER REPORT: Very poor - twisted front feet and long back feet.
Been hobbled at one stage. Brown/black fore hooves badly
mis-shaped.

WEIGHT ON ARRIVAL: ....Not weighed.

FIRST WORMED: ...5.7.75....................

SECOND WORMED: ...7.9.75..................

FIRST VACCINATION: ...26.11.75.......   For following dates see Veterinary Record

SECOND VACCINATION: ...13.1.76..............

41

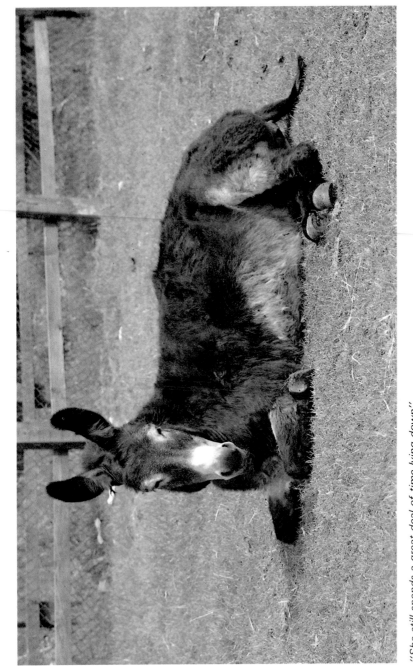

"She still spends a great deal of time lying down"

SUEY

Although the donkeys in Blackpool are well cared for, unfortunately, on other beaches they do not always fare so well and many have to be collected, exhausted from overwork and old age.

This was the case with Suey. The operator she worked for was one of the worst kind. Once the season was over, all the donkeys were 'turned away' — this means literally that they were herded into a rough field with no shelter and left to fend for themselves through the long winter. In Suey's group, an added complication was the fact that there was a stallion amongst the team. This meant all the younger mares, even those under two years old, inevitably got into foal.

Although the operator realised that Suey was elderly, he had not the knowledge to age her accurately by her teeth or he would have known that after the long hard winter she was well over thirty. Because of her age, she escaped the fate of the younger mares but when they were collected by the owner at Easter, she was very thin, and her feet, which had not been trimmed, were long and distorted.

One of the mares had indeed foaled in the February, and whilst she was made to give rides, the foal was kept on the beach as an attraction for the public.

Normally Suey had enjoyed giving rides, but this year she was almost exhausted before the season began. The saddles and bridles were too large, as they had previously been used for ponies. A piece of baler twine was used as a girth on the saddle, and this cut into her most cruelly. The bit had to be wired to keep it in place, causing sores on both her upper and lower jaws.

The end to Suey's ordeal came one hot July Friday in the first week of the children's school holiday. She had been giving rides almost non-stop since early morning, when a very large boy, well over the eight stone limit, insisted on riding her. Suey's knees buckled as he got on, but she got no sympathy from the operator who passed the boy his stick to 'make the b----r go!' It was on the return journey that her knees buckled and she slowly collapsed on to the soft sand. Despite frequent blows from the now angry operator, her eyes remained closed. Fortunately, the British public are animal lovers, and an angry crowd gathered. A rug was put over her by the operator as she was, in his words, 'spoiling the trade' and fortunately a bystander ran to the telephone and called the Sanctuary.

It was some hours before we got there, but as Suey was not fit to travel far, she spent the night with a supporter of the Sanctuary before undertaking the long journey to her new home.

When the wagon doors were opened and I climbed in to her, I was met with the dullest, saddest eyes I had ever seen. The driver had put all the supports up for her journey, as her feet were so badly distorted and she had very little strength of her own. Gently we helped her down the ramp, and her head lifted for a moment when she received the bray of welcome all new donkeys get on their arrival. Then she was led into her large airy box with a deep clean straw bedding, freshly shaken hay and cool clean water. Did I see just a little lifting of the head, a glint of interest in her eyes? By evening she was lying down, contentedly munching hay.

We left a full medical examination until the next day to give her time to recover. It was a very thorough veterinary check. She was thin, but not emaciated, and there was no sign of heart trouble or in fact anything to account for the long period of apparent unconsciousness. Perhaps she had just had enough. There were numerous sores and saddle galls which were treated every day, and after a week she had her equine flu inoculation and anti-tetanus jab and was treated for parasites. It took a great deal of time to get her feet back to normal and we all spent many hours with her, bathing feet and sores in rotation. Never once did she attempt to kick us, despite our ministrations, which must have been very painful at times.

Gradually she began to walk without pain and, without the cruel saddle and bridle, the sores began to heal and for Suey life became worth living again. She made friends with an elderly little mare called Jenny who moved in with her as her companion as soon as she was clear of lice and sores and had completed her isolation period. Donkeys are always better with a companion and with Suey we seemed to have a psychological as well as a physical problem to cope with. The cure worked wonders!

She still spends a great deal of time lying down. However, she is a happy donkey now thoroughly enjoying her richly deserved retirement.

The operator lost his licence and is no longer working. For your information, and in the interests of the donkeys you may be able to help, I will print here a simplification of the regulations relating to working donkeys. If you see these rules being broken, you can help the donkeys by reporting the operator to the local council office, where the operators' licences are issued, or by ringing the Sanctuary.

Every donkey must have at least one hour's rest mid-day for watering and feeding plus other short rests and NEVER stay on the beach more than nine hours in a day.

No one over 8 stone may ride a donkey.

Mares with young foals should not work.

No sticks should be used.

MISTY

DONKEY ADMISSION SHEET FOR THE DONKEY SANCTUARY, SIDMOUTH, DEVON

Computer Entry Date ....

DONKEY ADMISSION SHEET FOR THE DONKEY SANCTUARY, SIDMOUTH, DEVON

NAME: .....Misty............................ REF NO: ....

D.O.E. ....8.9.78........................ AGE: ....14 months..............

SEX: .....Stallion............. IF STALLION, GELDING DATE: ...11.1........

COLOUR AND DESCRIPTION: ....White and fluffy..............................

....

....

....

SINGLE/COMPANIONS: ....Single..

....

....

....

SOURCE OF ENTRY: ....Family will could no longer keep him - very much loved......

....

....

....

IF VIA D.S.I. INSPECTOR: ....,

GENERAL CONDITION ON ARRIVAL: Moderate

MEDICAL HISTORY/BACKGROUND, ETC: Said to be very distressed

FIRST VET REPORT: Heart sounds good.
Trachea and lungs moderate.

FARRIER REPORT: Good

WEIGHT ON ARRIVAL: ...125 kilos.....

FIRST WORMED: ....27.9.78...........

SECOND WORMED: ....20.12.78..........

FIRST VACCINATION: ...20.9.78...........

SECOND VACCINATION: ...3.11.78..........
For following dates see Veterinary Record

45

"Waiting for the next T.V. programme?"

MISTY

Donkeys are often accused of being noisy and there are occasions, defender of the donkey as I am, that I have to admit this! However, I justify them totally—there is always a reason.

Donkeys generally hate living alone; they love company of their own sort, and they love the company of people. As young animals, they are very active and play for hours. In the wilds of South America, I have watched feral herds, and the behaviour of the younger members of the herd is entrancing. During the cooler hours of the day, they form into groups and the young stallions will play out the battles which will become real in later life. They will spend an amazing length of time on their hind legs, forelegs locked round each other's shoulders, moving slowly around. The winner of the mock battle will often gallop off with a triumphant bray. Very often it is the lonely stallions who are the noisiest, and this was the reason why Misty joined us.

Misty had excellent owners—a kind caring family with children, who spent every spare moment with him. When Dad was gardening, there was always a carrot or a biscuit as he finished one chore and went on to the next and Misty would stand in his paddock watching him, quietly and happily waiting.

Unfortunately for Misty his paddock was surrounded by other houses, but as long as he could see activity in his house he was content. The problem came when the family wanted to go out. No sooner had the family car driven away than "Eeyore, eeyore", blared forth and the unfortunate occupiers of the other houses suffered until the family returned and peace was restored.

The family began to receive complaints, at first almost laughingly given, but gradually the atmosphere changed and Misty began to be an embarrassment. Then the family got their bright idea! When they had to go out they moved the television set to the lounge window overlooking the paddock and turned it on at half volume! The change was fantastic. Misty, with his chin propped on the rails, would follow every second of every programme, ears twitching, tail swishing, whether in approval or disapproval no one ever knew, until the family returned and he settled happily for the night, knowing his family were home.

The problem was then solved until September 1978. The family needed a holiday and, hoping against hope that Misty would be alright in the care of one of the now more friendly neighbours, the family left him, without the TV set!

To Misty the ensuing week was a nightmare. No family to talk to him and give him tit-bits. No television to watch. He quickly became frustrated, bored and finally naughty. He leant over the neighbours' fencing pulling out plants by the roots, he pushed at garden fences until they sagged, and he trotted round and round the field braying pathetically during the long hours of the night.

A deputation of grim neighbours met the family on their return—there could be no reprieve: Misty must go or the family leave.

A tearful call to us explained the situation and it seemed Misty was in need of help. We did point out that we could not offer a stable with TV, but we hoped the friendship of other donkeys would prove acceptable, and within 24 hours Misty had arrived.

There was no doubt the neighbours had a point. His bray was loud and a deafened unhappy family left him with us. After a few hours to get over the journey, he was introduced to Maxi with whom he became friends.

No donkey can remain a stallion at the Sanctuary, for obvious reasons, so five weeks after his arrival he was castrated. His family sent him 'a get well' card with a lovely message:—

"Hope you're feeling better now—
Much better every day,
So you will soon be well enough
To go outdoors to play!"

Misty did recover from his operation very quickly and, as so often happens, his temperament began to change from rampant stallion to quieter gelding. He began to take a great interest in his surroundings and loved the frequent visitors to the Sanctuary. His recovery box had high beams and it was amusing to see him let the hens and cockerels use his back as a half-way house to the rafters on their way up to safe perching at night.

Now Misty has grown from the young 15-month-old stallion on arrival to a handsome gelding. He is still with his friend on Brookfield Farm where he has many other companions and acres to play in. He doesn't need to bray anymore—he is never lonely and has quietened down and become a normal donkey. When they visit him, his family hardly recognise the quiet, happy, gentle donkey he has become — but I do notice a faraway look in his eyes when they pet him—perhaps he is thinking of the T.V. programmes he is now missing?

Hello! Feeling Better?

To Misty

Hope you're
feeling better now —
Much better every day,
So you will soon be
well enough
To go outdoors to play!

Always thinking of you,
from everyone
at Brentwood.
x x x

CHARLIE GIRL

DONKEY ADMISSION SHEET FOR THE DONKEY SANCTUARY, SIDMOUTH, DEVON

Computer Entry Date ....

DONKEY ADMISSION SHEET FOR THE DONKEY SANCTUARY, SIDMOUTH, DEVON

NAME: Charlie Girl .... REF NO: 1198 ....

D.O.E. 8.3.82 .... AGE: 12 ....

SEX: Mare .... IF STALLION, GELDING DATE: ....

COLOUR AND DESCRIPTION: Colour pink...................................
Probably in foal as has been with a stallion .....

SINGLE/COMPANIONS: Bambi and Minnie (her mother)..........................

SOURCE OF ENTRY: Purchased by a lady from a farmer in order to save them .....
being sent for slaughter ....

IF VIA D.S.I. INSPECTOR: ....

GENERAL CONDITION ON ARRIVAL: Fair

MEDICAL HISTORY/BACKGROUND, ETC: Kept all winter on disused railway line
with no shelter.

FIRST VET REPORT: Increased lung sounds - in foal

FARRIER REPORT: All overgrown

WEIGHT ON ARRIVAL: Not weighed ...

FIRST WORMED: 11.3.82 ....

SECOND WORMED: 14.4.82 ....

FIRST VACCINATION: 11.3.82 ....

SECOND VACCINATION: 27.4.82 ....

For following dates see Veterinary Record

ANGEL

DONKEY ADMISSION SHEET FOR THE DONKEY SANCTUARY, SIDMOUTH, DEVON

Computer Entry Date ....

DONKEY ADMISSION SHEET FOR THE DONKEY SANCTUARY, SIDMOUTH, DEVON

NAME: .....Angel....................... REF NO: ......1269.................

D.O.E. ...30.5.82....................... AGE: .....Born 30.5.82.........

SEX: .....Filly............... IF STALLION, GELDING DATE: ....

COLOUR AND DESCRIPTION: ....Brown/Gingery.....................................

....

....

....

SINGLE/COMPANIONS: ...With mother Charlie Girl..........................

....

....

....

SOURCE OF ENTRY: ....Born to Charlie Girl 1198...........................
.................at Slade House Farm.....................................

....

....

IF VIA D.S.I. INSPECTOR: ....

GENERAL CONDITION ON ARRIVAL:

MEDICAL HISTORY/BACKGROUND, ETC: Born to Charlie Girl who arrived in the
                                   Sanctuary in foal 8.3.82

FIRST VET REPORT:

FARRIER REPORT:

WEIGHT ON ARRIVAL: ....

FIRST WORMED: .....16.6.82...........

SECOND WORMED: ....

FIRST VACCINATION: ....

SECOND VACCINATION: ....

Charlie Girl, Bambi & Minnie on the disused railway line

Charlie Girl & Minnie arriving at the Sanctuary

CHARLIE GIRL AND ANGEL

Charlie Girl is one of those delightful donkeys who go straight to your heart!

I was in the office early on a Monday morning when I received a distress call from Somerset, where a donkey-lover poured out her sad story.

Near to her house was a disused railway line, fenced off from the fields around, still with the old cinder track on which grew a very pathetic crop of weeds and rough grass. A section of the line had been fenced off by a local farmer, and for the whole of the winter a stallion and three donkey mares had lived there with no shelter and, as far as she could ascertain, no food. She had managed to buy hay and feed for them, and every day had carried it to the hungry donkeys. That morning she had found the stallion gone. When she rang the farmer, she was told that the other three would also be going for slaughter for pet food. She was unable to contemplate such a fate for the mares, and she was also fairly certain that they were in foal. So she made the farmer a cash offer which he accepted, and she was now the desperate owner of the pathetic animals, with nowhere to keep them, as the farmer wanted them moved immediately.

Fortunately, I was able to contact our driver, who set off straight away. The rescuer's fears were very well founded. Thanks to her help in feeding, the bodily condition of the donkeys was reasonable, but they were certainly heavily in foal.

Gently they were introduced to a large airy stable and the bran mash with molasses which always seems heaven to donkeys! Charlie Girl was arrival number 1198 on the 8th March 1982. My goodness, they certainly ate enough for two. During the six-week new admissions isolation period they never stopped eating! In these six weeks, all donkeys have a full medical examination and are inoculated against equine flu and tetanus: they are also wormed. The farrier examines their feet. In short, this is the time when they get to know us — and we get to know them. This 'getting to know you' period is even more vital when the mares are in foal, as they need to have complete confidence in us in case of trouble. For many donkeys, it is the first time they have felt gentle hands and heard loving voices, and it is really wonderful to see how quickly they regain confidence.

Charlie Girl and I felt an unusual affection for each other immediately. She was a lovely strawberry roan colour and so gentle, despite her hard winter. I hoped she would have an easy labour.

After her isolation she went out into the 'Maternity Field' with her friends and Buttercup, the Jersey cow who was also expecting a calf.

On Friday, the 28th May, I noticed she was getting rather uncomfortable, so late in the evening I put her in a box of her own with an infra-red light wired up so that any new arrival could be cared for immediately. Despite her discomfort, and my frequent night visits, nothing happened, so out she went into the field again.

Saturday was a wonderful day for me, because at 6.30 p.m. Buttercup produced the dearest little heifer calf, chocolate brown, which we named 'May'. Having settled her comfortably, Jane the vet, and I both had a look at Charlie Girl, who once again looked unhappy.

It was when I checked at 4.45 a.m. that I got my reward. Charlie Girl was laid out panting, and the birth was just at the stage where help was possible and needed. A gentle pull and the little foal slithered out, all neatly wrapped in its membrane bag. I ripped it open, as Charlie Girl was exhausted, and then, laying the little foal by its mother's head, I gained the richest reward anyone can have: just watching a mother and baby together. Gently she began to lick it as it lay by her — the licking stimulating both of them. "You little angel," I murmured, touching the soft little white hooves, not even hard set yet. Slowly Charlie Girl sat up and Charlie's Angel, as she had become, began the struggle to get up on her shaking legs. In half an hour, both were standing. One wet little Angel, with back legs appearing far too long, busy trying to discover at which end Mother kept the milk bar! When I gently pushed her head towards the udder she had great difficulty in getting her head under it but at last she succeeded, and what a joy to hear the first sucking noise!

I left them both supremely happy with the infra-red light on. Angel was born seven weeks after her mother's arrival, and was the 1269th arrival in the Sanctuary. She was now assured of a permanent happy future with us. For Angel, there would be none of the hard railway tracks which had been poor Charlie Girl's former home.

Charlie Girl safe at last